A GUIDE FOR AUTHORS, TRANSLATORS AND COPY-EDITORS

IIIT STYLE-SHEET

THE INTERNATIONAL INSTITUTE OF
ISLAMIC THOUGHT
LONDON OFFICE

THE INTERNATIONAL INSTITUTE OF ISLAMIC THOUGHT
P.O. BOX 669, HERNDON, VA 22070, USA

LONDON OFFICE
P.O. BOX 126, RICHMOND, SURREY TW9 2UD, UK

ISBN 1-56564-282-1 paperback

Typesetting by Sohail Nakhooda
Cover Design by Shiraz Khan
Printed in the United Kingdom by
Oxuniprint at the Oxford University Press

CONTENTS

Note 5

I. The Production Process 7

1.1 Preliminaries 7

1.2 Acknowledgement of Receipt 7

1.3 Achieving a 'Sound Manuscript' 7

1.4 Copy-Editing 8

1.5 Preparing In-House Proofs 9

1.6 Marking-Up 10

1.7 First Page-Proofs 11

1.8 Revised Page-Proofs 11

1.9 'Repro' 12

1.10 Who Does What? 13

II. Guidelines for Authors 14

2.1 Know the Production Process 14

2.2 Know the Production Route 15

2.3 When E-Mail is the Only Route 16

2.4 Know the IIIT Style-Sheet 17

III. Guidelines for Translators 19

3.1 Qualifications for the Task 19

3.2 Definition of the Task 19

3.3 Enlarging the Definition 19

3.4 Evolving a Strategy 20

IV. Style-Sheet 24

4.1 American, Not British 24

4.2 Transliteration 24

4.3 The Use of Italics 28

4.4 Quotations 29

4.5 The Use of Initial Capitals 31
4.6 Use of Al-/The 33
4.7 Bibliographical Information: General 34
4.8 The 'Preferred Style' 35
4.9 The 'Author-Date Style' 42
4.10 Miscellaneous Matters 46

Appendix 1 American English Spellings 52
Appendix 2 Particular Spellings 54
Appendix 3 Transliteration Table 58
Index 61

NOTE

AUTHORS HAVE A STAKE in the final quality of work that bears their name. It is in their interest therefore to cooperate in making the production of their work as efficient as possible. Following a brief overview of successive stages in the production process which contains some account of the tasks of copy-editing and proof-reading, this booklet offers guidelines for authors and translators on how to prepare and submit their work. It also contains a style-sheet, a list of particular conventions or rules, which must be applied by authors, translators, copy-editors, and proof-readers alike.

The purpose of both the Guidelines and Style-sheet is the same – to standardize format across the full range of IIIT publications and so reduce costly re-working and delays in the production process. The booklet as a whole is the outcome of consultations among people with many years of experience in preparing publications. That said, it remains possible that a situation will arise (for example, technical material requiring unique production values and formats) in which the Style-sheet conventions must be relaxed or amended. In this case, the general rule is: explain the special requirement to the editor in charge of the project who will, after consultation, determine how best it can be met.

We are especially indebted to Dr. Jamil Qureshi for his extensive revision and addition to the work and extremely valuable recommendations and amendments made to the final draft. We would also like to thank all those who contributed throughout the years to the preparation of the original material: Rashid Messaoudi, Zaynab Alawiye, Shiraz Khan, Alexandra Grayson, Jay Willoughby, Imran Ahsan Nyazee, Dr. Riad Nourallah and Sohail Nakhooda.

IIIT/LONDON OFFICE
JANUARY 2002

DR. ANAS S. AL-SHAIKH-ALI
DIRECTOR, TRANSLATION DEPARTMENT

I
THE PRODUCTION PROCESS

ALTHOUGH AUTHORS and translators may be directly involved in this process only at the proof-reading stage, the rationale of the guidelines and conventions they are requested to follow will be much easier to implement if they are aware of the process as a whole.

1.1 PRELIMINARIES

IIIT will commission experts to assess, in confidence, work which has already been submitted or which is being prepared for publication. Following the referees' reports, the editor(s) will agree with the author(s) an outline description of the content, scope, length, level, and organization of the work. After the outline has been agreed, delivery dates and production schedules will be settled and, as appropriate, a formal contract will be issued. It expedites the process if, at this early stage rather than later, authors can alert the editor(s) to any questions of copyright that may arise: the time needed to secure the relevant permissions can sometimes be unpredictable.

1.2 ACKNOWLEDGEMENT OF RECEIPT

Once the manuscript in the agreed form has been delivered, the editor(s) will acknowledge receipt of it, noting clearly for the benefit of all parties whether the manuscript is complete – main text as well as academic apparatus (notes, bibliography, indexes, appendices, etc.) and any additional matter (maps, illustrations, tables, etc.) – and if not, listing the missing elements.

1.3 ACHIEVING A 'SOUND MANUSCRIPT'

The editor(s) may again, when necessary, refer the work to academic consultants to confirm that it broadly complies with the outline as initially agreed. Assuming it does, the editor(s) will then either pass the manuscript back to the author, or pass it on to a copy-editor, to refine the arrangement and presentation of the work in detail. It is at this stage that inadequacies or incompleteness in the references or elsewhere, accuracy of translations and quotations, etc., should be pointed out and made good. Any substantive changes to the work made by a copy-editor will normally be referred back to the author(s) for approval. Eventually, a 'sound manuscript' will be achieved. The major responsibilities of the author(s) or copy-editor at this stage are to ensure:

a. that the text is fluent and clear, free of unjustified technicality, ambiguity, obscurity, or vagueness;
b. that the argument is presented through well-constructed sentences, paragraphs, and sections, and builds in a coherent, consecutive way which readers (for whom the work is intended) can follow comfortably;
c. that allusions and references, names and dates and all other information, are as reliably accurate as possible;
d. that any quoted material and the sources indicated for it are given accurately;
e. that any translated passages are both accurate and useful, that is, the passage must not include so many untranslated terms or phrases that it ceases to function as a translation.

1.4 COPY-EDITING

The general aim of this stage is to make a 'final draft' out of the 'sound manuscript'. The principal tasks of the copy-editor are to ensure:

a. that the manuscript conforms fully and consistently to the conventions of the IIIT Style-sheet;
b. that notes and cross-references within the work function correctly (for example, information provided in references

in the footnotes must not conflict with the information provided for the same references in the bibliography; similarly, headings in the text and in the contents must correspond);

c. that heading levels are both clear and correctly and consistently formatted throughout the text;

d. that paragraph styles (for example, first paragraph after a heading, quoted extracts of prose or verse) are both clear and correctly and consistently applied throughout the text;

e. that character styles (for example, how a book title is abbreviated or a proper name spelled, or if/when a term is italicized) are both clear and correctly and consistently applied throughout the text;

f. that the text makes good sense. Clearly, this task belongs to the previous stage (achieving a 'sound manuscript'), but a fresh mind and eye may spot omissions or contradictions or other lapses that have been missed. Copy-editors should, if they feel competent to do so, suggest wording that may correct the error, and/or supply information that makes good any deficiency. The editor(s) will decide if the copy-editor's suggestions are to be accepted or referred back to the author(s) for further action.

1.5 PREPARING IN-HOUSE PROOFS

Normally, one copy of the 'final draft' will be sent to the author(s) to proof-read: however, in rare circumstances, production schedules and other practicalities may prevent this. One copy of the 'final draft' will be sent to a proof-reader who will incorporate the amendments (if any) submitted by the author(s). The principal responsibilities of the proof-reader are to ensure:

a. accuracy and consistency in spelling and punctuation;

b. accuracy and consistency in the formatting applied in the work as a whole and in its individual sections;

c. completeness of the text: accuracy of the pagination in the parts and the whole, the proper location of any additional materials (maps, illustrations, etc.), the accuracy of legends and captions and of cross-references within the work (for example, the functionality of such instructions as "see Fig. 8").

1.6 MARKING-UP

This is the later stage of proof-reading when a clean print-out of the 'final draft' is marked up for the compositor (typesetter). The print-out itself must indicate, or the proof-reader must indicate by handwritten notes, the following:

a. heading levels and styles, including spacing before and after, and fonts and font sizes;

b. paragraph styles, including spacing, fonts, conventions for superscripted and subscripted elements, footnote cues, etc.;

c. character styles used for emphasized or foreign words;

d. paragraph and character styles for captions and legends;

e. any special requirements (for example, additional characters that may be needed to accommodate foreign spellings; the desired location of illustrations in relation to text);

f. any special permissions (for example, if a particular illustration may be re-proportioned to suit the design of a page).

Note that, normally, compositors will have been informed beforehand of the paragraph and character formats needed for the particular work; and that, in any case, most requirements will be adequately signalled on the print-out by in-house word-processing. Therefore, marking-up is done for the sake of *additional* clarity, to prevent possible misunderstanding, and to provide helpful notes (see (e) and (f) above) where difficulties are anticipated.

It is good practice to use the same conventions as everyone else when marking up a manuscript. If unsure, refer to the list of marks and the sample text given on pp.112–13 of *The Chicago Manual of Style* (14th edn. Chicago: The University of Chicago Press, 1993).

1.7 FIRST PAGE-PROOFS

The proofs returned by the compositor, with the manuscript now set in the form of printed pages, will be checked by the proof-reader. It is desirable for author(s) also to check page-proofs. However, this will depend on production schedules, and editor(s) are required to give priority to maintaining schedules. In any case, substantial revisions at this stage are expensive and, except in the rarest of cases (for example to correct some 'terrible mistake' which ought never to have been missed), will be disallowed. Any amendments proposed by the author(s) must be incorporated by the proof-reader with his/her own amendments onto a single copy of the page-proofs which the editor will return to the compositor.

1.8 REVISED PAGE-PROOFS

This set of proofs (also called 'second proofs' or 'revises') will not (except by exceptional prior arrangement) be sent to the author(s), but handled in-house by the proof-reader. This is absolutely the last opportunity the production team has to ensure:

a. that typos (mistakes in spelling), mistakes in punctuation, mistakes in numbering of pages or maps or tables or other material, are marked up;

b. that line-endings are carefully checked so that any unacceptable hyphenations introduced during the process of justification of the text can be indicated;

c. that headers and footers run correctly and are properly aligned; that headings are properly connected to the following text (not, for example, separated by a page or column break or by an intervening illustration or table); that any 'loose lines' (i.e. lines in which the words are unevenly spaced) are marked up; that any 'widows' or 'orphans' (single lines appearing, respectively, at the bottom or top of a page, separated from the rest of the paragraph) are marked up; that any variations in font size or weight occur only where they are meant to occur;

d. that all illustrative and textual material for the covers and dust-jacket (if any) is correct. It is especially important to check elements (such as the blurb or abstract or other text to be used in advertising, and artwork commissioned separately from the main body of the publication) which will have entered the production process at a different time and run along a different channel.

1.9 'REPRO'

Reproduction proofs (or 'repro') are the final copy from which the work will be photographed and then printed. The only significant corrections that can be justified at this stage are gross errors which, if permitted to go through, would render the author(s) and/or IIIT liable to prosecution. Normally, only the editor will review repro, or designate someone else to do so, in order to confirm that amendments marked on the revised proofs have been put into effect and to signal any blemishes on the page. Corrections must never be marked on repro, but only on a photocopy thereof, and a separate list of the page numbers of the pages needing attention should be sent to the printer, along with the photocopies bearing the corrections.

The equivalent of repro for prints prepared from photographic negatives (given different names depending on the technical procedure involved) will, similarly, only be reviewed by the editor or designer or by someone deputed to take on the responsibility in their absence. Again, no significant changes are normally countenanced at this stage. However, if the editor judges that the image quality (tone, contrast, color, etc.) needs to be improved, the blemishes should be indicated on a photocopy of the 'original' sent by the printer. One of the reasons for using a photocopy is that marking the 'original' may obscure whatever needs attention.

1.10 WHO DOES WHAT?

There is no inflexible ruling about whether, for any individual project or series of projects, the editor, copy-editor, and proof-reader are one and the same person, or many. The advantages of a fresh mind and fresh pair of eyes going over the same text are self-evident. However, practical considerations to do with the availability of resources within particular production schedules will, usually, determine how work is allocated within the editorial team. That said, the overall production process remains the same, and the work must be formally checked through each stage before it is 'progressed' to the next.

II
GUIDELINES FOR AUTHORS

(In this section 'authors' is used to mean whoever submits work to IIIT for publication; in this sense, a translator is also an 'author'.)

2.1 KNOW THE PRODUCTION PROCESS

IT IS ESSENTIAL that prospective authors understand the production process outlined in the previous section. Making that process more efficient (which benefits all parties) is the rationale behind these guidelines.

Work must be submitted both in paginated typescript (so-called 'hard copy') and in electronic form on diskette (so-called 'soft copy'). Submitting work as an attachment to e-mail is not encouraged: the transfer process usually entails severe losses of formatting and characters. (However, see 2.3 below.)

Do not attempt to reproduce in your typescript the look of the printed page as you would like it to be, or by analogy with previous IIIT publications. Instead, present your work in a form that makes the task of the editors more straightforward:

a. Make a list of all the elements enclosed with a manuscript, such as maps, photographs, tables, etc., indicating the number of items in each category, just as you would indicate the number of pages of text. Doing this will enable the editor to confirm that the package as received is complete.

b. Print on only one side of the paper; use double spacing throughout. Indicate headings clearly as such, as well as the level of the heading – for example, chapter headings might be marked 'H1', section headings would then be

'H2', sub-sections 'H3', and so on. Leave a wide margin (at least two inches) on one side of the page to allow for readers' or editors' notes.

c. By far the greatest single source of problems in preparing a text for publication is unreliability, inconsistency or incompleteness of the academic apparatus. As editors cannot themselves supply the necessary information, they are obliged to engage in lengthy and frequent correspondence with authors which burdens and delays the production process. It is always worthwhile therefore, before submitting your work, to re-check the content of quotations, footnotes and sources for completeness and accuracy, as well as ensuring that the sources of **all** quotations are fully detailed in the footnotes. Similarly, re-check the bibliography and the glossary.

2.2 KNOW THE PRODUCTION ROUTE

By 'production route' we mean the computer operating-systems and software that are used between the electronic copy supplied by the author and the final, printed product. As the technology is evolving rapidly, and as it can be prohibitively expensive to keep up with it, we do not consider it practicable to insist on a single, fixed production route for IIIT journals or books. However, authors should be aware of the issue of compatibility of the WP (word-processing) package and (most especially) the typeface they are using, with those used in-house by IIIT and then by typesetters and printers commissioned by IIIT. It is, for example, most frustrating – for editors as well as authors – that authors' painstaking efforts to transliterate are annulled when the work is opened using a WP package or font that cannot convert the transliterated characters. Documents attached to e-mails are even more vulnerable to conversion difficulties and much of the formatting, as well as any special characters, may be lost in the process.

It is quite likely that software will soon become available that is both universal and reliable in its competence to reproduce typefaces and formats across different WP and operating systems. In the meantime, authors are requested to:

a. be aware that in-house preparation at IIIT of textual matter is currently done using the WP package Microsoft Word 2000 (for MAC or Windows operating systems) and that final output is produced using QuarkXPress for MAC;

b. indicate clearly in an accompanying letter or e-mail the name and version number of the WP software they have used, and any other information that might be helpful in attempting to convert it;

c. submit a hard copy which can serve as a 'master' against which any print-out from an electronic copy can be checked and corrected.

2.3 WHEN E-MAIL IS THE ONLY ROUTE

We appreciate that there are circumstances in which authors may have no practicable alternative to sending part (or whole) documents by e-mail, i.e. without hard copy or with hard copy 'to follow' after some (often unpredictable) postal delay. When e-mail is the only option, and MS Word or some other equally common and powerful WP package is not available to them, we would ask authors to send documents in Text Only format. The current practice among academics who correspond regularly by e-mail and need to indicate transliteration is as follows: use lower case throughout; double up vowels that are meant to be long; type the strong consonants in upper case; use apostrophe ['] for hamzah; use the grave accent [`] for ʿayn; thus:

ā ī ū would be typed: aa ii uu
ʿumalā' would be typed: \`umalaa'
ḍ ḥ ṣ ṭ ẓ would be typed: D H S T Z

Example

The name Muṣṭafā Maḥmūd would be typed muSTafaa maHmuud

The title *al-Ḥikmah fī Makhlūqāt Allāh* would be typed al-Hikmah fii makhluuqaat allaah

There are obvious limitations to this 'solution' – the non-use of upper case in any Arabic words and phrases, and the absence of formatting (such as italic). However, it has the merit of simplicity and reliability, and a relatively straightforward Find and Replace operation can be used by IIIT staff to convert characters into the desired form.

A less popular, but also effective, 'solution' is to underline the characters (including \` and ' for ʿayn and hamzah) that are meant to be transliterated. This is a slower method but, since underlining is a fairly stable format that usually survives the e-mail process, just as reliable. The same examples as above using this method would appear thus:

Example

The name Muṣṭafā Maḥmūd would be typed Mustafa Mahmud

The title *al-Ḥikmah fī Makhlūqāt Allāh* would be typed al-Hikmah fi Makhluqat Allah

2.4 KNOW THE IIIT STYLE-SHEET

Authors should make themselves familiar with the conventions listed hereafter in the Style-sheet, and apply those conventions consistently when preparing their work for submission. Authors' cooperation in this matter will, by reducing unnecessary labor during the editorial process, contribute significantly to improving both the quality and quantity of IIIT publications.

The conventions are self-explanatory as listed. Here, we would urge authors to give special attention to the following:

1. The list of words which must be spelled in a certain way regardless of usage elsewhere. (See Appendix 2, pp.54–57 below.)
2. The rationale and the rules of transliteration (4.2.1, and Appendix 3). In particular, when the names of persons are to be transliterated and when not (4.2.1(c)).
3. The order of items to be supplied in references in footnotes, and in references in the bibliography; and the punctuation used to separate these items (4.8.1–3).
4. How to give references in footnotes in the 'long' and 'short' styles (4.8.2–3).
5. How to indicate long quotations or 'excerpts' (4.4(b)).
6. How to indicate quotations from the Qur'an (4.4(f), (g)).
7. The use of single and double quotation marks (4.10.5).

III
GUIDELINES FOR TRANSLATORS

3.1 QUALIFICATIONS FOR THE TASK

THE IDEAL TRANSLATOR will have native user competence in the target language (say, English) and be highly proficient in the language he or she is translating from (say, Arabic). In addition, he or she will need to have (or to acquire) considerable skill in the subject-matter of the work being translated, and be competent to deploy that skill in *both* languages, as a reader in the source language and as a writer in the target language.

3.2 DEFINITION OF THE TASK

The task of translation must be strictly distinguished from scholarly edition, annotation, critique, etc. The translator, as a translator, must not omit or interpolate passages, nor paraphrase or otherwise alter the original. On the contrary, he or she must render the original faithfully and comprehensively, with the minimum possible changes in form or substance. Such minimal changes are justified by the need to achieve naturalness, clarity, and fluency in the translation. It is best to regard the task as a trust, a duty of service to the work being translated. The translator may opt to do *more* than present the original faithfully in a different language. But that primary duty must be discharged first.

3.3 ENLARGING THE DEFINITION

With the agreement of the editor responsible for the project, the translator may provide, either in a separate introductory essay, or in footnotes to the translation, additional material (comments or notes) as appropriate.

a. If, as sometimes happens, a classical text is being translated, the most authoritative edition of the original will be used. However, that edition may have opted, here and there, for a reading which makes less sense to the translator than the reading in another, generally less authoritative, edition. In this case, the 'inferior' reading must be translated in the main text with a footnote indicating and translating the alternative ('better') reading.

b. Where the text makes very difficult sense, it may be appropriate to offer an explanatory paraphrase in a footnote.

c. Where it is necessary to supply many words in the translation that (for whatever reason) do not reflect what is found in the original text, the necessary interpolation must be written within square brackets (see 4.4(c)), and an explanatory footnote provided.

3.4 EVOLVING A STRATEGY

A general understanding of the original is not sufficient preparation for the task of translation. It is prudent to identify and then tackle points of difficulty in the original before sitting down to write out a draft of the translation. Without a clear strategy adequate to deal consistently and coherently with the difficulties, the translation will proceed by *ad hoc* solutions and, sooner or later, falter. Then, portions of the work may have to be completely re-done or discarded.

Since each project will present its own, unique set of challenges, it is impracticable to prescribe detailed rules for how challenges should be met. However, on the basis of past experience, a number of points are always worth keeping in mind. In broad terms, the challenges a translator faces fall into two categories, the mechanical and the literary/linguistic:

3.4.1 *Mechanical Difficulties*

a. In any text, old or modern, the translator will need to identify quotations. If these quotations are in fact paraphrases, they must be translated as such but a note explaining the fact should be provided. In some texts, the quotations may be translations from works originally written in the target language or some other language. Those works must be identified, and, if need be, the quotations must be re-translated from their original into the target language. (Self-evidently, translating a translation is an invitation to error.) Note that references in the original text to translated works may, in the translation, become references to the originals of those translations: the bibliography must be amended accordingly.

b. Some of the works quoted in the original will, of course, have been written in the same language as the original (most obviously, for works in Arabic, the Qur'an and Hadith). If reliable translations of such works already exist in the target language, it is preferable to use them rather than re-translate. Any works so used must be listed in the bibliography.

   However, bear in mind that the quoted words may have been interpreted or given an emphasis special to the context of the work under translation. Then, the translator must check that the emphasis intended by the author is, at the very least, not contradicted by the existing translation of the quoted words. If there is a conflict, a new translation must be attempted.

c. Spelling of place-names and names of persons must, in the translation, conform to the conventions of the Style-sheet. Therefore, it will be necessary to identify, and arrange access to, the relevant reference works (biographical dictionaries, geographical and historical atlases, etc.) to get the spelling right.

d. References in the original, in its notes and in its bibliography, must be adapted to conform to the relevant conventions of the Style-sheet. It is particularly important that the items of information needed in references are as complete as practicable, and are written out in the right order.

3.4.2 *Literary/Linguistic Difficulties*

Besides individual passages likely to be difficult to express in the target language, translators should try to identify: (a) recurrent words or phrases; (b) words or phrases that function as technical terms; (c) peculiarities in the language of the original which enable the argument to be structured or expressed the way it is; (d) stylized mannerisms that characterize the particular writer and/or literary genre of the work. The next stage is to consider options to deal with the difficulties:

a. How does context affect the meaning of the recurrent words and phrases? Can one word or phrase in the target language be used to translate every instance of the same word in the original? If not, what degree of variation in rendering that word is appropriate? And should the reader be alerted to the fact in notes or an introductory essay?

b. What equivalents (if any) are there for the technical terms in the original? The translator should refer to comparable subject-matter in the target language to find equivalent terms, or at least to see how that language handles similar or related topics. He or she may then be able to select words which, though not ordinarily technical, can convey the delimited sense needed in the context.

c. Words in every language trail a host of cultural associations which users of that language share. This makes it possible to convey meaning by wordplay, implicit allusions, etc. For example, by choosing a turn of phrase that echoes a familiar hadith or verse of the Qur'an, the writer may add an important level of meaning to the point being made. It is almost never possible to reproduce this kind of device in a different language. But it may be desirable to alert the reader to the effect the author intends. More generally, it is important to ask what level of knowledge or training readers of the original are assumed to have. If a great deal is assumed, will it be necessary to clarify this in an introduction and/or suggest further reading? Or will it suffice to clarify such devices, as it were, locally, in footnotes?

d. How far is it possible to reflect the original's stylized mannerisms in the target language, and how consistently? Usually it is not possible to do so *and* retain naturalness or ease in the translation. It then becomes important to decide whether these mannerisms, peculiar to the author or the genre or the epoch of the work, are a substantive part of its meaning or a formal device (a courtesy) used to establish a particular kind of relationship between author and reader. If the latter, it may be wiser to describe this aspect of the work in an introductory note, and explain why it would be inappropriate to attempt to translate it.

IV
STYLE-SHEET

THE RULE OF RULES is consistency. At a number of points in this Style-sheet two equally acceptable conventions are indicated. This does not mean that the two different conventions may be used randomly in the same work. On the contrary, only one of the two equally acceptable ways must be adopted and then followed consistently. Whenever an alternative is offered, it must be understood as an either/or choice, not an and/or choice.

4.1 AMERICAN, NOT BRITISH

a. IIIT publications follow standard American (U.S.) conventions, rather than British. For example, in modern British practice, an abbreviated word is not followed by a full-stop if the abbreviation contains the last letter of the word; thus ed. (for editor) but eds (editors) and edn (edition). The American practice is to retain the full-stop; thus: ed. (editor), eds. (editors), edn. (edition).

   For all matters not covered by this Style-sheet, and when in doubt on any point, authors and copy-editors should refer to preferably the latest edition of *The Chicago Manual of Style* (Chicago: University of Chicago Press).

b. Similarly, IIIT publications follow American English and not British English spelling. A list of commonly used words that differ in the two systems is given in Appendix 1 (p.52 below).

4.2 TRANSLITERATION

Words and proper names of Arabic origin or written in a script derived from Arabic must sometimes be 'transliterated', sometimes 'partly transliterated' (or 'corrected'), and sometimes (usually in the case of names of persons and places) the spelling as found must be accepted just as it is – 'untransliterated'. By way of illustration, some examples of how the same word would appear in, respectively, transliterated, partly transliterated, and untransliterated form:

Qur'ān – Qur'an – Koran
ᶜulamā' – ᶜulama – ulema
Muḥammad – Muhammad – Mohammed

A transliteration table, showing the Arabic characters and the Latin characters used to represent them, along with some rules to clarify usage, is given in Appendix 3 (p.58 below).

4.2.1 *To Transliterate, or Not*

a. The rationale of transliteration is to enable readers to work out, from the form of the transliterated word, the original Arabic. This, in turn, enables them to look up the word, the person's name, the book title, etc., in the appropriate reference work. That is why transliteration follows (as closely as reasonably practicable) the script rather than the sound of Arabic. (For example, we say: '*ash-shamsu wa-l-qamar*', but we write: *al-shams wa al-qamar.*)

b. Problems arise because, to meet immediate everyday needs, people transliterate the sound rather than the script. Also, as people hear sounds differently, and different languages indicate quite similar sounds by different combinations of the same letters, a bewildering array of spellings of the same word can be found in use. The problem is most acute with names of persons but it arises also with common nouns that have entered into usage in Western languages and are recorded in standard dictionaries, and with place names recorded in standard atlases.

c. The rule to be followed is this: Where the Arabic of a common noun or the name of a person or place has become established in a particular form in English, that established form must be used in preference to any other. The reason for this preference needs to be understood. If a work of the well-known author Fazlur Rahman is attributed to 'Faḍl al-Raḥmān', readers will have difficulty locating the work in a standard library catalogue. Similarly, if Dar es Salaam/Darussalam is written as Dār al-Salām, some readers may not know that a particular city is being referred to, those who do may not know how to find it in the index of a standard atlas.

d. Exceptions to the rule will be extremely rare for names of persons or places (see Appendix 2(a), p.54). However, numerous exceptions to the rule need to be made for common nouns. The two good reasons for this should be understood. (1) Some established spellings are particularly misleading, and IIIT publications must contribute to the process of correction. For example, the spelling 'Muslim' is steadily displacing the incorrect 'Moslem'; 'Ramadan' is steadily displacing the incorrectly rendered 'Ramadhan' or 'Ramazan'. (2) Some words of Arabic origin are, even if not yet recorded in all standard dictionaries, so widely used in English that it would be unreasonably pedantic to insist on treating them as foreign words.

e. Common nouns whose established spelling is to be corrected (point 1 in the preceding paragraph), and common nouns in the process of becoming standard usage (point 2), make up a special group of 'partly transliterated' words. The list is given in Appendix 2(f) (p.56 below). Note that none of these words is classed as 'foreign', and therefore none is italicized. Note also that some 'corrected' words must always be written with an initial capital (Appendix 2(b), 2(d–e)).

f. Some English dictionaries give two or more variant spellings for the same word. In this case, use the more correct form. For example, the spelling 'qāḍī' is to be preferred to 'cadi'.

g. If an established spelling (as defined for the rule in (c) above) is such that an Arabic speaker might not recognize the word, give the correctly transliterated form of the word in round brackets after the first occurrence of the misleading spelling. For example: muezzin (*mu'adhdhin*).

h. Following the rule as given in (c) above, the names of the prophets must be given in the established English spelling. However, to prevent errors of identification, give the Qur'anic name in round brackets after first occurrence of the English name. For example: Noah (Nūḥ).

i. Any quoted text must be quoted as it is, always, without amendment. However, a potentially misleading or incomprehensible spelling may be corrected (as explained in (g) above), this time in square brackets (see 4.4(c)).

Bibliographical information (author name, title) should be quoted from the title-page of the publication. Therefore the rule for quoted text applies.

j. In rare cases, two spellings of the same author name may have to be quoted in the same bibliographical listing. This will happen if publications in Arabic and publications in English by the same author are listed in the same place. It can also happen when older translations of the work of an author (in which the name is rendered into English haphazardly) and later translations (in which the same name is transliterated correctly) are listed consecutively. To retain both spellings could lead to the misconstruction that there are two different authors. Therefore, in such cases, prefer the correctly transliterated form but give the other spelling in round brackets after it. For example: al-Mawdūdī (Mawdoodi).

4.3 THE USE OF ITALICS

a. Italics must not be used as a heading style for main headings. Italics may be used as a character style, within headings, to distinguish particular elements within the heading. For example: 'The development of *uṣūl* in Iraq'.

b. Italics must not be used for Arabic or other words of foreign origin defined in this Style-sheet as having entered common usage. See the list in Appendix 2(b), (d–f) (pp.54–57 below).

c. Italics may be used as a character style for other foreign words, not defined as in common usage, or for words which, in a particular publication, are used in a special technical sense. Generally, avoid the use of italics whenever possible.

d. Italics may be used sparingly as a character style to indicate emphasis.

e. When giving bibliographical information, italics must be used for the titles of books and journals. (Emphasis within the title is therefore indicated using roman characters.)

f. When giving bibliographical information, italics must not be used for the titles of articles in journals, the titles of chapters, the titles of essays in multi-author publications, or the titles of unpublished papers or dissertations. Similarly, italics must not be used for the names of authors or publishers, nor for the place or date of publication.

g. Italics must not be used for the names of persons or places, except to indicate special emphasis (as (d) above).

h. Italics must not be used as a general style for quotations, whether the quotation is short or long, verse or prose. However, italics may be used as a character style within a quotation to indicate emphasis (as (d) above).

4·4 QUOTATIONS

a. In general, short quotations (less than three lines) must be enclosed within double quotation marks and set within the main text. Only exceptionally – for reasons of special emphasis, or because the quoted text demands special layout – may short quotations be set off from the main text.

b. Long quotations or 'excerpts' (three lines or more) must be set off from the main text as a distinct paragraph and indented from both the left and right margins. Do not use italics or quotation marks to indicate 'excerpts'. When an author's typescript is set in preparation for final printing, the layout ordered for 'excerpts' may require a smaller font and full measure (i.e. no indentation). However, author typescripts must indicate 'excerpts' by indenting from both margins.

c. Interpolations within quotations (to clarify the sense or for some other reason) must be enclosed within square brackets.

d. Ellipses (omissions from quoted text) must be indicated by three consecutive unspaced dots, and without the addition of spaces either side of the dots.

e. Quotations from the Qur'an may be selected from one or more reliable, existing translations in order to give the accurate rendering that best suits the context in which the Qur'anic text is being quoted. In general, archaic forms ('thee', 'ye', etc.) in existing translations must not be reproduced. However, exceptionally, in the context of comparing two or more translations, the original must be cited (following the rule 4.2.1(i)) without amendment.

f. Quotations from the Qur'an will normally be indicated by citing surah and verse number(s) in round brackets, i.e. (2:238) rather than (*surat al-Baqarah*: v.238) or (The Qur'an, Chapter 22 verse 238) or other variations. The surah and verse numbers must be separated by a colon without space on either side. To indicate a range of numbers use the en dash; multiple references must be separated by a semi-colon, not a comma. The full stop (period) of a sentence that ends with a short Qur'anic quotation is written **after** the brackets surrounding/including the Qur'anic reference, not before the closing double quotation marks. Examples:

> *Surat Saba'* says: "My reward shall come from none but God. He is the Witness over all" (47).
>
> Or elsewhere in the Qur'an, God says: "We test all of you with good and evil, and to Us you shall all return" (*al-Anbiyā'*: 35).

g. The divisions of the Qur'an must be designated by the terms surah (**not** chapter) and verse (**not** *āyah*). In referring to individual surahs, the name of the surah must be transliterated and italicized and preceded by the word *Surat*. Examples:

> In *Surat Yūsuf*... (**not** In surah *Yūsuf*...)
> In *Surat al-Nisā'*... (**not** In *al-Nisā'*...)

4.5 THE USE OF INITIAL CAPITALS

a. The names and attributes of God, the name Allah itself, and pronominal forms referring to God (He, Him, His; Who, Whom, Whose; and on occasion, We, Our when Allah speaks of Himself), must always have an initial capital. Examples include:

the All Knower, the Most Merciful
the Oneness of God, His Omnipotence, His Mercy
His Hand, His Throne

b. In personal names which are composed with the name Allah, and which it is permitted to transliterate (see rule 4.2.1(c)), 'Allah' must be written as a separate word with an initial capital. For example: ᶜAbd Allah (**not** ᶜAbdallah or ᶜAbdullah).

c. The word 'ibn' when it is a medial element within a personal name must be written without an initial capital. However, when the name is abbreviated so that 'ibn' becomes the initial element of the name, it must be written with an initial capital. Moreover, 'ibn' should not be transliterated as 'bin'.

Ibn Taymiyyah or Aḥmad ibn Taymiyyah

d. The word 'abū' when it forms part of a transliterated personal name must always be written with an initial capital. For example: Abū Muṣṭafā.

Note that in the construct state 'abū' becomes 'abī', and if it occurs in this form within the Arabic name being transliterated, the inflection must be indicated. For example: ᶜAlī ibn Abī Ṭālib.

Sometimes the 'abū' is not inflected because of a relationship with another part of the name, but because of its relationship with a word outside the name (in the example following, it is governed by the preposition *lī*). In this case the inflected form is not indicated:

He said to Abū Muṣṭafā (*qāla lī Abī Muṣṭafā*).

e. The word 'prophet(s)' must be used without an initial capital unless it is immediately followed by the proper name, or occurs in the phrase 'the Prophet' which is now universally understood to mean 'Prophet Muhammad'. Examples:

All the prophets brought the same message.
The Prophet said . . . Prophet Muhammad said . . .

(Note that use of the definite article with both the title and name together sounds awkward in English – by analogy with a phrase like 'the King John' which is incorrect. Therefore constructions like 'the Prophet Moses' should be avoided.)

f. The names of the months of the Islamic calendar and the names of sects and dynasties must always be written with an initial capital. Similarly, 'Islam' (meaning the religion), 'Muslim' (meaning one who has embraced Islam), 'Shariʿah' (meaning the Islamic Law), 'Revelation' (meaning the Qur'an), must be written with an initial capital. Certain words or phrases that, in special contexts, function as proper nouns (for example: 'the Last Day', 'the Hour'), must be written with an initial capital. (Most of the words mentioned in this paragraph which are of Arabic/Qur'anic origin form a sub-set of the 'partly transliterated' words explained earlier. For an extended list, see Appendix 2(b–c), pp.54–55 below.)

4.6 USE OF AL-/THE

Use or omission of the definite article (*al-*/the) before a common noun must follow the rules of grammar of the language in which it occurs.

a. For common nouns which name something that is considered unique, it is necessary in English to write 'the', as in (for example) 'the New Testament'. Therefore, for analogous instances of single Arabic nouns used in an English phrase or sentence, we may translate the Arabic *al-* literally, as in 'the Qur'an', 'the Sunnah', 'the Kaʿbah'. In such cases, 'the' must replace *al-* and not be added to it:

   the Qur'an (**not** al-Qur'an, **not** the al-Qur'an)
   the Sunnah (**not** al-Sunnah, **not** the al-Sunnah)
   the Kaʿbah (**not** al-Kaʿbah, **not** the al-Kaʿbah)

b. For common nouns which name something that is neither defined by being unique, nor defined in the context, the definite article is not permitted in English. Therefore, for analogous instances of single Arabic nouns used in an English phrase or sentence, *al-* must not be translated. For example:

   Modern developments in Islamic jurisprudence . . . (**not** the Islamic jurisprudence)
   Modern developments in *fiqh* . . . (**not** the *fiqh*)

   In the same way, honorific titles (al-Imam, al-Shaykh) used as part of the name of a person must not have the definite article when rendered in English. For example, al-Imam al-Shāfiʿī must be written Imam al-Shāfiʿī.

c. For common nouns occurring within an Arabic phrase, the whole of which is being used in an English sentence, *al-* must be retained since it is required by the rules of grammar governing the Arabic phrase. Examples:

   Uṣūl al-Fiqh al-Islāmī

   al-maṣāliḥ al-mursalah

   al-Khulafā' al-Rāshidūn

   Ahl al-Kitāb

   Special care will be needed, when using whole Arabic phrases, to avoid repeating the definite article of the Arabic in English. For example, *Ahl al-Kitāb* already means 'the People of the Book'; a construction like 'the *Ahl al-Kitāb*' is therefore absurd. In order both to retain naturalness in English and avoid the absurdity, it may be preferable in some instances to translate the phrase and give the Arabic in parentheses.

d. 'Al' should always be written with a hyphen linking it to the word it defines. When typing, a non-breaking hyphen should be used to ensure 'al' remains on the same line as its partner. Moreover, the definite article should always be written as 'al', never as 'ul' or 'il', irrespective of the grammar of the sentence, word, or phrase being transliterated.

4.7 BIBLIOGRAPHICAL INFORMATION: GENERAL

There are two styles in general usage, the so-called 'humanities style', and the 'author–date style'. Each has its distinct merits and advantages, but the 'humanities style' (hereafter referred to as the 'preferred style') is preferred for IIIT publications. The 'author–date style' is convenient, compact and reliable, but it is most suited to strictly academic work intended for a narrower readership than many IIIT publications. Moreover, it can only be used in conjunction with a formal bibliography appended to the work. For shorter publications, and for publications intended for inclusive readership, a formal bibliography is not always appropriate.

Within either style, it is necessary to distinguish the conventions for references as given in a formal bibliography, and references as given in footnotes/endnotes. There are important differences in the number of items required and, more particularly, in the order in which the items are presented.

Within the 'preferred style' only, it is also necessary to distinguish within footnotes/endnotes, 'long' and 'short' references used, respectively, for first and subsequent references to a work.

4.8 THE 'PREFERRED STYLE'

4.8.1 *The Items of Information Required*

The items of bibliographical information required are listed below. Note that all the items listed are not necessarily available for every publication mentioned in a work, but must be supplied when available.

a. Author(s) name(s) – main name(s), first name(s) and/or initials.

b. Other authorship information – where relevant, such information as 'editor', 'translator', etc.

c. Title – the title of publication (book, journal, etc.), article or essay or chapter title, volume and issue number for journals.

d. Additional information – where relevant, information about additional elements within a publication with distinct authorship, e.g. 'Foreword by . . . '

e. Publication details – publisher's name, place of publication; where relevant: name of series, number of volumes; date of publication or 'no date' (and, where relevant, specification of the calendar).

4.8.2 *Presentation of the Information: Examples*

As explained above, the items of information required, the order of presentation and, to a lesser extent, the punctuation used to separate the different items, varies according to whether a reference is presented in the bibliography proper, or in 'long' or 'short' references in footnotes/endnotes. The examples that follow (one or two are fictional) have been selected to illustrate, consecutively, each of the three forms of presentation for a sufficient variety of publications to cover most eventualities. The examples are preceded by the letters B, L, or S, to mean, respectively, 'Bibliography', 'Long reference', 'Short reference'. We urge authors and copy-editors to be particularly attentive to the punctuation used to separate the individual items of information.

Example 1

B Beck, Aaron T., *Cognitive Therapy and the Emotional Disorders*. New York: New American Library, 1976.

L Aaron T. Beck, *Cognitive Therapy and the Emotional Disorders* (New York: New American Library, 1976), pp.29–35.

S Beck, *Cognitive Therapy*, pp.32–33.

Example 2

B Badri, Malik B., 'Abū Zayd al-Balkhī: A Genius Whose Contributions to Psychiatry Needed More Than Ten Centuries to be Appreciated', *Malaysian Journal of Psychiatry* 6(2) (September 1999), pp.48–53.

L Malik B. Badri, 'Abū Zayd al-Balkhī: A Genius Whose Contributions to Psychiatry Needed More Than Ten Centuries to be Appreciated', *Malaysian Journal of Psychiatry* 6(2) (September 1999), pp.48–53.

S Badri, 'Abū Zayd al-Balkhī', p.51.

Example 3

B al-Ghazālī, Abū Ḥamīd, *Al-Ḥikmah fī Makhlūqāt Allāh*. Beirut: Dār Iḥyā' al-ʿUlūm, 1984.

L Abū Ḥamīd al-Ghazālī, *Al-Ḥikmah fī Makhlūqāt Allāh* (Beirut: Dār Iḥyā' al-ʿUlūm, 1984), pp.13, 14.

S Al-Ghazālī, *Al-Ḥikmah*, p.17.

Example 4

B al-Ghazālī, Muḥammad, *Fiqh al-Sīrah*. Beirut: Dār al-Kutub al-Ḥadīthah, 1960.

L Muḥammad al-Ghazālī, *Fiqh al-Sīrah* (Beirut: Dār al-Kutub al-Ḥadīthah, 1960), p.190.

S Al-Ghazālī (Muḥammad), *Fiqh al-Sīrah*, p.191.

Example 5

B Elkadi, Ahmed, 'Quranic Concepts for Eliminating Negative Emotions: Another Aspect of the Healing Effects of the Quran'. Unpublished paper presented at the 5th International Conference on 'The Scientific Signs of Quran and Sunnah', Moscow, September 1993.

L Ahmed Elkadi, 'Quranic Concepts for Eliminating Negative Emotions: Another Aspect of the Healing Effects of the Quran' (unpublished paper: Moscow, September 1993).

S Elkadi, 'Quranic Concepts' (unpublished paper).

Example 6

B Carson, R.C., J.N. Butcher and J.C. Coleman, *Abnormal Psychology and Modern Life*, 8th edn. London: Scott, Foresman & Co., 1988.

L R.C. Carson et al., *Abnormal Psychology and Modern Life* (8th edn. London: Scott, Foresman & Co., 1988), p.368.

S Carson et al., *Abnormal Psychology*, p.368.

Example 7

B Ibn Taymiyyah, *Majmūᶜ Fatāwā al-Imām Aḥmad ibn Taymiyyah*. 24 vols. Riyadh: Maṭābiᶜ al-Riyāḍ, n.d.

L Ibn Taymiyyah, *Majmuᶜ Fatāwā al-Imām Aḥmad ibn Taymiyyah* (Riyadh: Maṭābiᶜ al-Riyāḍ, n.d.), vol.10, pp.221–25.

S Ibn Taymiyyah, *Fatāwā*, vol.10, p.221.

Example 8

B al-Albānī, Muḥammad Nāṣir al-Dīn, *Nasb al-Majānīq lī Nasf Qiṣṣat al-Gharānīq*. Beirut: Manshūrāt al-Maktab al-Islāmī, 1372 AH (1952).

L Muḥammad Nāṣir al-Dīn al-Albānī, *Nasb al-Majānīq lī Nasf Qiṣṣat al-Gharānīq*. (Beirut: Manshūrāt al-Maktab al-Islāmī, 1372 AH / 1952), pp.187–93.

S Al-Albānī, *Nasb al-Majānīq*, p.195.

Example 9

B Winter, T. J. (trans., with introduction and notes), *The Remembrance of Death and the After Life (Book XL of Iḥyā' ʿUlūm al-Dīn)*. Cambridge: Islamic Texts Society, 1989.

L T. J. Winter, (trans., with introduction and notes), *The Remembrance of Death and the After Life (Book XL of Iḥyā' ʿUlūm al-Dīn)*, (Cambridge: Islamic Texts Society, 1989), p.64.

S Winter, *Remembrance of Death*, pp.64–67.

Example 10

B Badri, Malik, *Contemplation: An Islamic Psycho-Spiritual Study*. Trans. from the Arabic by Abdul-Wahid Lu'lu'a; Introduction by Shaykh Yusuf al-Qaradawi. Herndon VA: International Institute of Islamic Thought, 2000.

L(a) Malik Badri, *Contemplation: An Islamic Psycho-Spiritual Study* (Herndon VA: International Institute of Islamic Thought, 2000), pp.13–15.

L(b) Malik Badri, *Contemplation: An Islamic Psycho-Spiritual Study* (Herndon VA: International Institute of Islamic Thought, 2000), 'Introduction' (by Yusuf al-Qaradawi), pp. ix–xi.

S Badri, *Contemplation*, p.18.

4.8.3 *Notes on the Examples*

a. In the bibliography, publication details are written as a separate sentence and not in parentheses. This is because the very function of the bibliography is to provide such information so that the work may be identified and ordered efficiently. In 'long' references, however, publiction details are not the focus of attention, and parentheses are used to enable readers (if they so wish) to 'skim over' the publication details.

b. For the bibliography, where works are listed by author name in alphabetical order, the author's main or identifying name must be given before his/her first name(s) or initials. For the 'long' references this order is reversed, and for 'short' references, usually only the main name is given. Note that, where confusion might arise, the first name must be given (compare Examples 3S, 4S).

c. For purposes of alphabetical sorting in the bibliography, an initial ᶜ*ayn* in an author's identifying name, and the article *al-*, are ignored. Because there is focus, in the bibliography, on alphabetical order, the *al-* is not written with an initial capital. However, in 'short' references where *al-* is the opening element in the sentence, it is written with an initial capital (compare Examples 4B/4S, 5B/ 5S).

d. Where there are more than two authors, use 'et al.' in both the 'long' and 'short' references, but not in the bibliography where all the author names must be given in full (see Example 6).

e. Where additional information about authorship is exceptionally long (see Example 10), it is best to provide it in a separate sentence before the sentence giving publication details. It is not usually necessary to give this information even in 'long' references (see 10L(a)). Very rarely, if the reference is specifically to the additional material in the work, the necessary minimum of information must be provided (see 10L(b)).

f. Do not give page references for unpublished material which is not bound and paginated (see Example 5). Page references should, of course, be given to bound and paginated dissertations held in university libraries or otherwise accessible to readers.

g. Depending on the nature of the subject-matter and the intended readership, it may be helpful to translate titles of works which are not in English. In this case, in the bibliography only (i.e. not in the references in notes) the English translation of the title may be given after the title of the original, in parentheses and in roman characters, not italics, and without quotation marks.

4.8.4 *Ibid. and other Abbreviations in References*

a. The abbreviation 'ibid.' meaning 'in the same place' must always have a full-stop after it. It will have an initial capital (Ibid.) if it opens a sentence. If a page reference is given as well, use a comma.

Examples

Badri, *Contemplation*, pp.16–18.

Ibid., p.19. (= the work cited in the preceding note, page 19).

Ibid. (= same work and same page as in preceding note).

b. The abbreviation 'op.cit.' is not to be used. Instead, use the 'short' reference style illustrated in 4.8.2.

c. The abbreviation for page is 'p.' The plural (pages) is 'pp.'

d. The abbreviation for volume is 'vol.' The plural (volumes) is 'vols.'

e. The abbreviation for (foot)note is 'n.' The plural (notes) is 'nn.'

f. Volume numbers must always be given in Arabic numerals, not Roman. The Roman style has no function except to create an impression of monumentality; it consumes space; and, in any case, most readers need to 'translate' into Arabic numerals to understand the number meant. For the purpose of locating the work in catalogues, it causes no difficulty to present the Roman numerals as Arabic ones.

g. A range of numbers (for volumes, pages or notes) must be separated with an en dash, not a hyphen, without space on either side of the dash. References in series to the same work must be separated by a comma. References in series to different works must be separated by a semi-colon.

Example

Ibn Taymiyyah, *Fatāwā*, vol.1, pp.221–25, vol.2, p.197; Ibn al-Qayyim, *Miftāḥ*, p.180.

h. Note that the abbreviations vol., p., n., are not separated by a space from the numbers that follow. However, when the numbers following must be given in Roman numerals, a space is used to prevent confusion:

Example

Badri, *Contemplation*, 'Introduction', pp. ix–xii. (**not** pp.ix–xii)

4.9 THE 'AUTHOR-DATE STYLE'

We emphasize that this is not the style used in most IIIT publications.

A brief description is offered here for the benefit of copy-editors or authors who may need to convert references and bibliography done in the 'author–date style' to the 'preferred style'.

a. There is no difference in the two styles in the items of information required.

b. The 'author-date style' is dependent on a formal bibliography which gives all the information needed, so that references in the text and in the notes can be very economical. In fact, there is no need at all for footnotes or endnotes which give the reader only bibliographical information.

c. Because this style is primarily intended for the use of academic readers, references to volume and page are not used. The convention is 'volume number: page number(s)'.

d. In the 'author–date style', in place of the difference between 'long' and 'short' style references, there is a difference between references within the text and references within notes.

e. Where two or more publications by the same author appeared in the same year, the identifying letters a, b, c etc., are added to the year in lower case.

f. Unless otherwise specified, a number after 'author–date' always means page number. Therefore, if a particular volume is being referred to without specification of page numbers within that volume, the abbreviation 'vol.' is used.

g. For ancient or classical works, reference by 'author–date' can look rather odd. For example, the reference 'al-Ghazālī 1988' will more readily bring to mind a modern author with that name rather than the great scholar–theologian Abū Ḥamīd al-Ghazālī. In some publications, therefore, the editor's name if appropriate, or the word 'edn.' after the year-date, are used to alert the reader. For works with no publication date, the abbreviation 'n.d.' is used in place of the year-date. However, if there are many such works attributed to the same author, it is advisable to provide identifying information, for example the place of publication.

h. In the illustrative examples following (all are fictional), the letters B, N, T are used to indicate respectively, information as presented in the bibliography, in references in notes, and references within the main text. Again, particular attention should be paid to the punctuation used to separate items of information.

Example 1

B Beck, Aaron T., (1976) *Cognitive Therapy and the Emotional Disorders*. New York: New American Library.

N For a detailed discussion see Beck 1976, pp.29–35.

T Both earlier and later discussions of this point (e.g. Beck 1976, 32–33; Badri 1999, 48–51) have stressed . . .

Example 2

B Badri, Malik B. (1999) 'Abū Zayd al-Balkhī: A Genius Whose Contributions to Psychiatry Needed More Than Ten Centuries to Be Appreciated', *Malaysian Journal of Psychiatry* 6(2) (September), 48–53.

N For a detailed discussion see Badri 1999, 48–53; 2000, 23–31.

T Badri in particular (1999, 48) has stressed that . . .

Example 3

B al-Ghazālī, Abū Ḥamīd (1984 edn.) *Al-Ḥikmah fī Makhlūqāt Allāh*. Beirut: Dār Iḥyā' al-ʿUlūm.

N For the classical Sunni viewpoint see al-Ghazālī 1984 edn., 13, 14.

T Al-Ghazālī (1984 edn. 13–24) was one of the earliest exponents . . .

Example 4

B Elkadi, Ahmed (1993) 'Quranic Concepts for Eliminiating Negative Emotions: Another Aspect of the Healing Effects of the Quran'. Unpublished paper presented at the 5th International Conference on 'The Scientific Signs of Quran and Sunnah', Moscow, September 1993.

N For an analogous approach, see Elkadi 1993.

T Elkadi (1993) makes a comparable claim for the healing . . .

Example 5

B Carson, R.C., J.N. Butcher and J.C. Coleman (1988 edn.) *Abnormal Psychology and Modern Life*, 8th edn. London: Scott, Foresman & Co.

N On particularly alarming aspects of the statistical evidence, see Carson et al. 1988 edn., 368.

T Carson et al. (1988 edn.) has been a standard text for some years.

Example 6

B Ibn Taymiyyah (n.d.) *Majmūᶜ Fatāwā al-Imām Aḥmad ibn Taymiyyah.* 24 vols. Riyadh: Maṭābiᶜ al-Riyāḍ.

N Ibn Taymiyyah offers the same line of argument in other similar rulings (see n.d., 10:221–25, 234–35).

T Ibn Taymiyyah (n.d., 10:221) is almost unique in his insistence on . . .

Example 7

B Badri, Malik (2000) *Contemplation: An Islamic Psycho-Spiritual Study*. Trans. from the Arabic by Abdul-Wahid Lu'lu'a; Introduction by Shaykh Yusuf al-Qaradawi. Herndon VA: International Institute of Islamic Thought.

N(a) The concept is elaborated further in Badri 2000, 13–15.

N(b) The healer's ambition is succinctly stated in Badri 2000, 'Introduction' ix–xi.

T Badri (2000, xiii) identifies some of the difficulties facing the translator who . . .

4.10 MISCELLANEOUS MATTERS

4.10.1 *Special Abbreviations*

The following special abbreviations may be used (in upper case and in brackets) as indicated:

(SWT) – at first mention of the name of Allah.
(ṢAAS) – at first mention of Prophet Muhammad.
(RAA) – at first mention of the name of a Companion.

4.10.2 *Acronyms*

An acronym may be used after the first occurrence of the name it is used to replace. It is easier to understand if the name is supplied before the acronym is used, rather than the other way around. For the sake of variety, an abbreviated form of the name may be alternated with the acronym, once it is clear what the acronym stands for.

Example

> The International Institute of Islamic Thought (IIIT) was set up . . .
>
> The IIIT now has offices in London and Islamabad . . .
>
> The Institute has an extensive publications programme, as well as . . .

4.10.3 *Dates*

For Gregorian or Common Era dates, it is not usually necessary to specify the calendar. However, when a date is given according to the Islamic or Hijri calendar and this date stands alone, the date must be followed by the letters AH written in small capitals and without full-stops. In any context where it is necessary to specify the Gregorian calendar, use the letters AC (**not** AD, **not** CE) or BC as appropriate. When dates from both calendars are given side by side, separate them with an oblique or forward slash (**not** with a hyphen or en dash). A range of dates in either calendar must be separated with an en dash (**not** a hyphen). When a range of dates is given side by side with a range of dates in a different calendar, separate the two ranges (as before) with an oblique or forward slash.

Examples

> Al-Ghazālī (d. 1111)
> Al-Ghazālī (d. 505 AH)
> Al-Ghazālī (d. 505/1111)
> Al-Ghazālī (450–505/1058–1111)

4.10.4 *Hyphens and Dashes*

A hyphen is used to join two elements which, when joined, form a single word or concept: for example, 'socio-economic', 'neo-Georgian'. By contrast, the en dash (about the length of two hyphens) is used to join two elements which temporarily form a single unit of attention, but do not make up a single word or concept: for example, 'the Iran–Iraq war', 'the London–Edinburgh train'. It is for this reason that the en dash is used to indicate a range of page numbers, or a range of dates: for example, '1914–1918', pp.8–12.

The em dash (about the length of three hyphens) must not be used. To indicate parentheses in a sentence (when brackets will not do), or to separate an explanatory comment from the main part of the sentence, use the en dash with a space either side.

Example

> He could not understand – or, more likely, did not choose to understand – the questions put to him.
>
> He remained silent – in other words, he refused to cooperate.

4.10.5 *Quotation Marks*

When quoting a phrase or sentence within the main text, use double quotation marks. When a word or phrase is marked to indicate that it is a coinage or is being used in a special sense, use single quotation marks. As an example we may quote a sentence used in 4.7 above:

"There are two styles in general usage, the so-called 'humanities style', and the 'author–date style'."

Note that, following American (U.S.) rather than British conventions (see 4.1), any punctuation used with double quotation marks must come inside the latter, not outside.

Example

"Xxxxx xxxx xxxx." (**not** "Xxxxx xxxx xxxx".)

4.10.6 *Titles with Personal Names*

As noted earlier, the article used in Arabic titles which form an established part of the name with which someone is remembered or addressed, must not be translated. In many cases, such titles as 'Doctor' or 'Professor' are not integral to the name of the person; and indeed in most other cases as well, they can and should be dropped.

The words 'brother' and 'sister' when used before a particular name must be written with initial capitals. In all other instances, the words (whether in singular or plural) must not be written with an initial capital.

Examples

Brother Omar. Sister Fatima.

My dear brother(s) and sister(s), you are most welcome.

4.10.7 *Punctuation Marks and Spacing*

After punctuation marks (comma, semi-colon, colon, full-stop, etc.) a single character space suffices. Do not use two or more spaces after such marks.

The paragraph style for 'excerpts' or long quotations has already been explained (see p.29). Except to ensure that paragraphs are clearly distinct from each other, and that headings and heading levels are somehow distinguished (if necessary by hand) on the typescript, authors have no responsibility for layout matters. As explained earlier, it is best to leave matters of layout to the editors and copy-editors who will be given instructions particular to each project or to each series of projects.

4.10.8 *The Hamzah and the Apostrophe*

The hamzah is transliterated by an apostrophe ['] or by a specially designed mark that resembles an apostrophe. Inevitably therefore, it will happen that the apostrophe is needed at the end of a word which ends with a transliterated hamzah. However, since the apostrophe is normally used before an 's' to indicate possession or some similar relationship, it is always preferable to re-write the word or phrase using an 'of' construction or a passive form to evade the apostrophe-s.

Example

> The *fuqahā'*'s ruling on this question, given at the 1986 convention . . .
>
> The ruling of the *fuqahā'* on this question, given at the 1986 convention . . .
>
> The ruling given on this question by the *fuqahā'* at the 1986 convention . . .

4.10.9 *Use of Brackets*

Use round brackets to enclose within a sentence any item of additional information (for example, the Arabic word that is only approximately expressed by an English equivalent; or the date of an event) which is not grammatically connected to the enclosing sentence.

Use square brackets to enclose any interpolations within quoted text and substantial interpolations within translated text.

If it becomes necessary to use brackets within brackets, use square within round, and round within square.

If the words enclosed within brackets form an independent

sentence, put a full-stop before the closing bracket. If the words enclosed within are part of another sentence, put the full-stop outside the closing bracket at whatever point the sentence ends.

4.10.10 *Consult the Manual*

There are a great many matters of substance and detail that are not touched upon in this Style-sheet. We have not sought to be comprehensive, but only to focus sufficient attention on those things that have in the past most perplexed authors and copy-editors who have worked with IIIT publications. Readers of this booklet are therefore reminded that, if they need a full and comprehensive discussion of the many difficulties that arise in preparing textual material for publication, they should consult *The Chicago Manual of Style* to which we referred above (1.6; 4.1(a)).

APPENDIX I

AMERICAN ENGLISH SPELLINGS

American (U.S.) English spellings must be used in all IIIT publications. A list of some of the most common words spelled differently than in British English is given below. For definitive rulings on U.S. spellings, refer to the Webster dictionary:

behavior
benefit, benefiting, benefited
caliber
center
color, coloring, colored
cooperate/cooperation
defense (noun), defenseless
dialog/dialogue
epilog/epilogue
favor, favorable, favoring, favored
flavor, flavored
fulfill, fulfilling, fulfilled
gray (**not** grey)
honor, honorable, honoring, honored
installment
jail (**not** gaol)
judgment
labeled
level, leveling, leveled
marvelous
meager
meter, centimeter, kilometer etc.

modeling
offense (noun)
practice (verb and noun), practicing
program
signaled
skeptic(al)
skillful, skillfully, skillfulness
succor
unraveled
valor
worship, worshiping, worshiped, worshiper

N.B. Many words that may end in either -ize or -ise in British English should be written with -ize in American English.

e.g.	specialize	specialization
	civilize	civilization
	immunize	immunization

Another general rule is that words ending in -our in British English usually take an -or in U.S. English.

e.g.	favor
	flavor
	color

APPENDIX 2

PARTICULAR SPELLINGS

For a variety of reasons, IIIT publications insist upon a particular way of spelling certain words.

2(a) *Specially Distinguished Names*

The name Allah, the name Muhammad when referring to the Prophet, and the names of Islam's two holiest cities should be written thus:

Allah (**not** Allāh)
Muhammad (**not** Muḥammad or other variant spellings)
Makkah (**not** Mecca, **not** Makkah al-Mukarramah)
Madinah (**not** Medina, **not** Madīnah al-Munawwarah)

2(b) *Common Nouns of Arabic Origin, Unique Referent*

Common nouns of Arabic origin which have a unique referent are written with initial capitals and, in most contexts, will take the definite article:

the Qur'an (**not** Koran, Quran, Qur'ān); (adjectivally) Qur'anic (**not** Koranic, etc.)

the Sunnah (meaning the Sunnah of the Prophet)

the Shariʿah (meaning the Islamic Law)

the Hadith (meaning the whole corpus of hadiths*)

the Kaʿbah (meaning the shrine in Makkah)

the Ummah (meaning Muslims or Muslim society in their entirety)

the Hijrah (meaning the hijrah of the Prophet from
Makkah to Madinah)

2(c) *Common Nouns, Not of Arabic Origin, Unique Referent*

Common nouns not of Arabic origin (but mostly translations of Arabic/Qur'anic concepts) which, by virtue of their meaning, have a unique referent are therefore written with initial capitals and will, in most contexts, have the definite article:

the Revelation (meaning the Qur'an)

the Law (meaning the Shariᶜah)

the Garden (meaning Paradise)

the Fire (meaning Hell)

the Last Day, the Day of Judgment

the Hour, the Day (meaning the Last Day)

Note the following terms which function as place names and so have initial capitals but not the definite article: Paradise, Heaven, Hell. Note also that a number of apparently very similar terms function as ordinary nouns and have neither definite article nor an initial capital: heavens (=skies), hellfire, hereafter, universe, earth.

2(d) *Months of the Islamic Calendar, Festivals*

Names of the months of the Islamic calendar, and the names of the two Islamic festivals, are written with initial capitals, but not italicized nor fully transliterated:

Muharram
Safar
Rabiᶜ I
Rabiᶜ II
Jumada I
Jumada II

Rajab
Shaᶜban
Ramadan
Shawwal
Dhu al-Qaᶜdah
Dhu al-Hijjah
ᶜId al-Fitr
ᶜId al-Adha

2(e) *Names of Schools, Sects, Dynasties*

As a general rule, the names of juristic and theological schools, sects and dynasties that have entered into general usage are not transliterated or italicized, but must have initial capitals. A few examples only are given:

Muᶜtazilites (**not** Muᶜtazilah)
Umayyads (**not** Umawiyyūn)
Abbasids (**not** ᶜAbbāsiyyūn)
Ottomans (**not** ᶜUthmāniyyūn)
Kharijites (**not** Khawārij), etc.

In the context of a technical discussion, and in any instance where an Arabic speaker might not recognize the word that is intended, the word correctly transliterated may be given in brackets or indicated in a footnote.

2(f) *Common Nouns of Arabic Origin, in General Usage*

Common nouns of Arabic origin that have entered into general usage are not italicized, nor written with initial capitals or diacritical marks, other than ᶜ :

ᶜalim*
dhikr
fatwa*

fiqh
hadith*
hijrah
hajj
ijmaʿ
ijtihad
imam*
jihad
jinn
mufti*
qiblah
salah
surah*
zakah

*Words marked with an asterisk appear in some English dictionaries and may therefore be made plural by adding -s: ʿalims, fatwas, etc.

APPENDIX 3

TRANSLITERATION TABLE

1. CONSONANTS

b	ب	ṭ	ط
t	ت	ẓ	ظ
th	ث	ʿ	ع
j	ج	gh	غ
ḥ	ح	f	ف
kh	خ	q	ق
d	د	k	ك
dh	ذ	l	ل
r	ر	m	م
z	ز	n	ن
s	س	h	ه
sh	ش	w	و
ṣ	ص	y	ي
ḍ	ض		

2. VOWELS

a) *Short Vowels*

(i)	a	فتحة َ	(ii)	a	همزة بالفتح «أَ»
	u	ضمة ُ		u	همزة بالضم «أُ»
	i	كسرة ِ		i	همزة بالكسر «إِ»

b) *Long Vowels*

ā	اَ	e.g.	*ḥarām*	حَرَام
ū	وُ		*rasūl*	رَسُول
ī	يِ		*dīn*	دِين
ā	الف مدة «آ»		*ādāb*	آداب
ā	الف مقصورة «ى»		*Mūsā*	مُوسَى

3. DIPTHONGS

ay	يَْ	e.g.	*bayt*	بَيْت
aw	وَْ		*yawm*	يَوْم

4. HAMZAH

Except when it appears at the beginning of a word (in which case, treat as per (a)(ii) above), *hamzah* is transliterated by using an inverted comma: '. Some examples are given below.

(i) *Medial forms:*

sa'ala	سَأَلَ
ra'ā	رَأَى
ra's	رَأْس
as'ilah	أَسْئِلَة
ḍa'īl	ضَئِيل
mi'dhanah	مِئْذَنَة
mu'min	مُؤْمِن
ru'ūs	رُؤُوس
murū'ah	مُرُوءَة

(ii) *Final forms:*

qara'a	قَرَأَ
ashyā'un	أَشْيَاءٌ
bad'an	بَدْءاً
hanī'an	هَنِيئاً
fuqahā'u	فُقَهَاءُ
yajī'u	يَجِيءُ
ḍaw'un	ضَوْءٌ

5. FURTHER POINTS TO NOTE

a. The definite article *al-* must be joined with a non-breaking hyphen to the word it defines. For example: al-Bukhārī; *al-qamar.*

b. Nouns with the feminine ending must be written *-ah*, not *-a*. But when the word is the first element of an *iḍāfah* construction, the final *tā' marbūṭah* must be made more explicit by writing *-at*. For example, Madīnat al-Nabī (**not** Madīnah al-Nabī). However, if the word is an element in an adjectival construction (where both words have the definite article), the ending remains *-ah*. For example: *al-dawlah al-islāmiyyah.*

c. *Shaddah* is generally represented in English by doubling the consonant above which the symbol appears. For example: Muhammad, hajj. However, where an Arabic sun-letter at the beginning of a word takes *shaddah* when preceded by *al-*, this is not reflected in the transliteration. For example: *al-Raḥmān al-Raḥīm* (**not** *al-Rraḥmān, ar-Raḥmān* or *arraḥmān*). Moreover, when a noun ends in *yā'* with *shaddah*, it is simply transliterated as *ī*. For example, *āyat al-kursī* (not *āyat al-kursīyy*).

d. Adjectives: use *-i/ī* for masculine words, and *-iyyah* for feminine words. For example: *al-kitāb al-ᶜarabī*; *al-maktabah al-islāmiyyah.*

e. *Tanwīn* (nunation) is represented, where necessary, by the word endings *-an*, *-in*, or *-un*, or, in the case of *tā' marbūṭah*, as *-tan*, *-tin*, or *-tun*.

f. The Arabic word for 'and', *wa*, is always written in full and without a hyphen after it, and any following *al-* is not elided. For example: *al-shamsu wa al-qamaru biḥusbān* (**not** *al-shamsu wa'l-qamaru*); *Zaynab wa Fāṭimah* (**not** *Zaynab wa-Fāṭimah*).

INDEX

abbreviations, 24, 41, 46–47
abu, correct use of, 31–32
acronyms, 47
adjectival construction, 60
Allah, 31, 54
Allah, names of, 31
alphabetical sorting, 40
amendments, 9
American spellings, 52–53
apostrophe, 50
author-date style, 42–46
authors
    et al., use of, 40
    knowing the production process, 14–15
    responsibilities of, 8
ʿayn, 16–17, 40

bibliographies, 34–35
    alphabetical sorting, 40
    author-date style, 34
    examples, 36–39, 44–46
    humanities style, 34
    items required in, 35–36
    punctuation, 36
    use of italics, 28
brackets, 50–51

character styles, 10
    italics, 28–29
Chicago Manual of Style, 11, 24, 51
classical works, 43
Common Era dates, 47
common nouns
    of Arabic origin, 56–57
    with definite article, 33
    transliterating, 25–26
    with unique referent, 54–55
compositors, 10
context, 22
conventions for marking up manuscripts, 10
copyright, 7

dashes, 48
dates, 47–48
definite article, 32, 33–34, 60
dynasties, 32, 56

ellipses, 29
em dash, 48
e-mail, 16–17
    avoiding sending work by, 14
    loss of formatting, 15–16
emphasis, 29
en dash, 48
endnotes, 35
et al., use of, 40
excerpts, 29

festivals, 55–56
first page-proofs, 11

footnotes, 35
  abbreviation of, 42
  importance of re-checking, 15
full-stops, 24, 30

God, names of, 31
Gregorian dates, 47

hamzah, 16–17, 50
hard copies, 14
heading levels, 10, 14–15
Hijri calendar, 47
honorific titles, 33
hyphens, 48

ibid., use of, 41
ibn, correct use of, 31
iḍāfah construction, 60
images, 13
in-house proofs, 9
initial capitals, 31–32, 55
interpolations, 29
italics, 28–29

long references, 35, 36–39

MAC operating system, 16
manuscripts, 7–8
  marking-up, 10–11
Microsoft Word 2000, 16
months in Islamic calendar, 32, 55–56
Muhammad (the Prophet), 32, 54

names
  abu, correct use of, 31–32
  composed with the word Allah, 31
  ibn, correct use of, 31
  of God, 31
  of prophets, 27
  of schools, sects and dynasties, 32, 56
  translations, 21–22
  transliterating, 25–26
  variant spellings, 27
  with titles, 49
nunation, 60

op.cit., 41

page, abbreviation of, 41
page-proofs, 11–13
paragraph styles, 10
partial transliteration, 25, 26
place-names, 21–22
preliminaries, 7
production process, 7–13, 14–15
project roles, 13
pronouns referring to God, 31
proof-readers, 9–10
prophets, 27, 32
publication details in bibliographies, 39–40
punctuation, 36, 44, 49–50

QuarkXPress, 16
quotation marks, 48–49
quotations, 29–30
  correcting misleading spellings in, 27
  importance of re-checking, 15
  in translations, 21
Qur'an, quoting from, 29–30

receipt, acknowledgement of, 7
references
  et al., use of, 40

ibid., use of, 41
in translations, 21–22
long and short, 35, 36–39
unpublished material, 41
reproduction proofs, 12–13
revised page-proofs, 11–12
roles in a project, 13

schools of thought, 56
second proofs, 11–12
sects, 32, 56
short references, 35, 36–39
soft copies, 14
sound manuscripts, 7–8
spacing, 49–50
spelling, 24, 26, 52–53
square brackets, 27, 50
styles, 10

tanwīn, 60
technical terms, translating, 22
Text Only format, 16
titles (honorific), 33, 49
titles (of works), translating, 41
translation
linguistic difficulties, 22
mechanical difficulties, 21
strategies, 20
titles of works, 41
translators, qualifications of, 19
transliteration, 24–28
partial transliteration, 25, 26
table, 58–60
when using e-mail, 16–17
typesetters, 10

underlining, 17
unpublished material, 41

volume, abbreviation of, 41

Windows operating system, 16
word processing packages, 15–16

Errata

Page	*For*	*Read*
17, lines 20-21	Mustafa Mahmud	Mustafa Mahmud
17, line 23	Al-Hikmah fi Makhluqat Allah	Al-Hikmah fi Makhluqat Allah
30, line 11	Chapter 22	Chapter 2
59, line 7	Dipthongs	Diphthongs
59, line 13	inverted comma	apostrophe